Collins
Big Cat
Picture
Dictionary

Consultant: Cliff Moon

Look for my balloon and my paw prints on every page!

Collins Big Cat Picture Dictionary

First published 2006

© HarperCollins*Publishers* Ltd 2006

10 9 8 7 6 5 4 3 2 1

ISBN-13 978-0-00-721405-1
ISBN 0 00 721405 7

A catalogue record of this book is available from the British Library.

Published by Collins
A division of HarperCollinsPublishers Ltd
77–85 Fulham Palace Road
Hammersmith
London W6 8JB

Browse the complete Collins Education catalogue at:
www.collinseducation.com

www.collins.co.uk

Consultant Cliff Moon

Cover designer Anna Stasinska
Design Anna Stasinska

Editor Jennifer Steele

Illustration: Big Cat cartoons: pp1-64 Michael Renouf; pp6-9 Nick Schon; pp10-11 Gary Dunn; pp12-13 © Tony Blundell; pp14-15 © Trevor Dunton; pp16-19 © Tony Blundell; pp 20-21 Mike Phillips; pp22-23 © Trevor Dunton; pp24-25 Melanie Sharp; pp 26-27 © Tony Blundell; pp28-29 Beccy Blake; pp30-31 Lisa Williams; pp32-33 Nick Schon; pp34-35 © Kelly Waldek; pp36-37 Lisa Smith; pp38-41 Charlie Fowkes; pp42-43 Lisa Williams; pp44-45 Melanie Sharp; pp46-47 Lisa Smith; pp48-49 Gary Dunn; pp50-51 Lisa Williams; pp52-53 © Kelly Waldek; pp54-55 Beccy Blake.

Printed by Printing Express Ltd, Hong Kong

Contents

How to use this dictionary

It's fun to learn new words with Big Cat and **Collins Big Cat Picture Dictionary**.

Looking and talking

Open the dictionary. Look at the big picture in the middle of the page. What can you see?

There are lots of things to look for and talk about. Can you answer Big Cat's question?

Don't forget to help Big Cat find his lost balloon and to look out for his paw prints!

The answers to Big Cat's questions are on page 64.

Finding new words

There are lots of exciting places to explore.

1. Let's find words about the beach. Look at the contents page to find *At the beach.*

2. *At the beach* is on page 32. Turn to page 32.

3. You want to find the word **crab**. The word **crab** begins with **c**.

4. Look around the picture. Run your finger down the page until you find words beginning with **c**.

5. You can also use the pictures to help you.

Contents

place   page number

picture

word

Using the topic pages

You can find lots of useful words on the topic pages.

Go to pages 48 to 55 to find words for opposites, shapes, colours, numbers, animals, time words and words we use a lot.

Opposites

asleep — awake

big — small

clean — dirty

come — go

dark — light

fast — slow

few — many

front — back

full — empty

heavy — light

high — low

hot — cold

loud — quiet

52

Using the index

The A–Z index tells you where you can find every word in the dictionary.

1. Let's find the word **inventor**.

2. The word **inventor** begins with the letter **i**. Look through the index until you find the section beginning with **i**.

3. Run your finger down the index to words beginning with **in**. Can you find **inventor**?

4. The word **inventor** is on page 10.

5. Turn to page 10 and run your finger down the words until you find **inventor**.

words beginning with i

word

Ii
I   55
ice cream   32
ice cream van   32
ice lolly   32
icy   43
in   55
in front   53
injection   21
insects   54
inventor   10
iron   6
is   55
island   34
it   55

Jj
jacket   41
jam   44

Ll
ladder   12
ladybird   31
lake   31
lamb   29
lamp   9
last   53
laugh   46
lawnmower   25
lawyer   36
lead   22
leaves   25
leg   38
lemon   19
letter   9
librarian   37
library   14, 16
lifeguard   32

59

page number

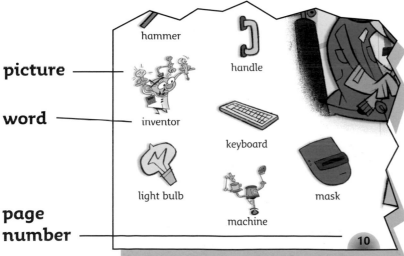

picture

word

page number

hammer

handle

inventor

keyboard

light bulb

machine

mask

10

See you inside!

At home

Where do you clean your teeth?

bath

bin

bowl

chair

cloth

cooker

cup

door

fire

fork

fridge

glass

iron

kettle

knife

light

bathroom

living room

matches

microwave

mirror

oven

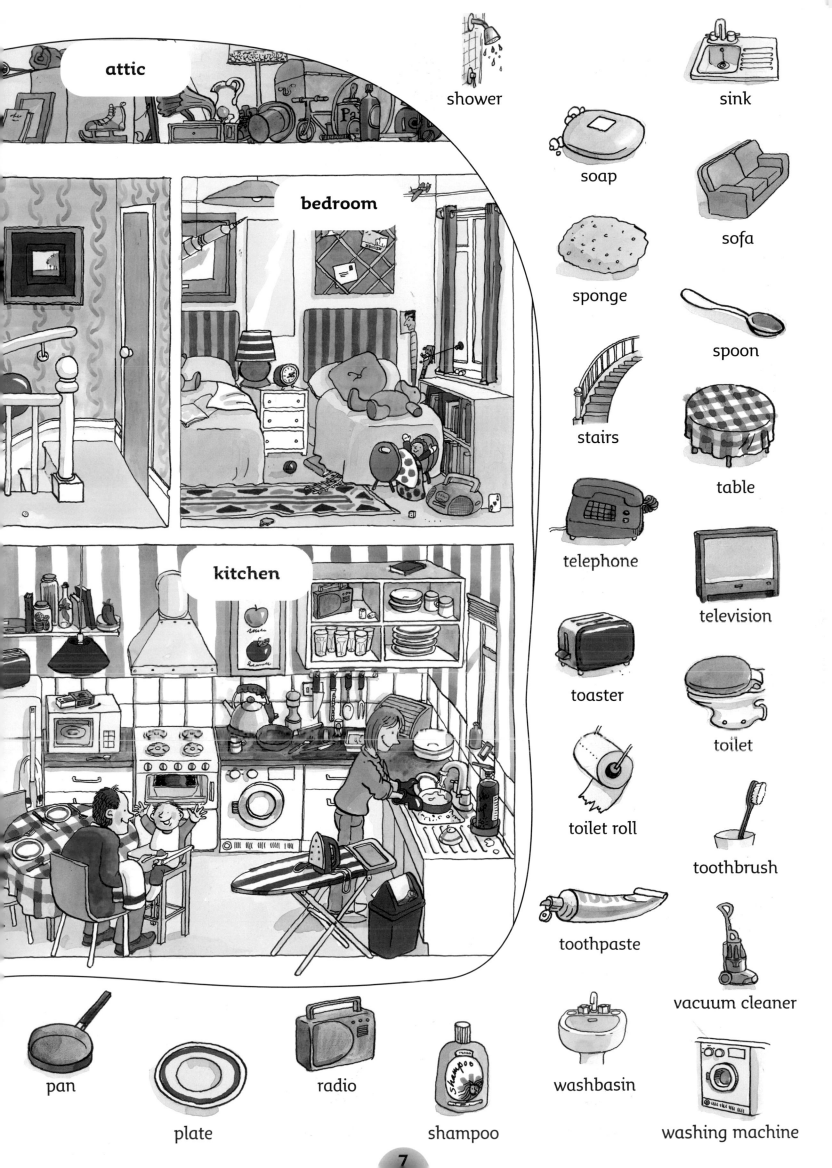

attic

bedroom

kitchen

shower

sink

soap

sofa

sponge

spoon

stairs

table

telephone

television

toaster

toilet

toilet roll

toothbrush

toothpaste

vacuum cleaner

washbasin

pan

plate

radio

shampoo

washing machine

In the bedroom

bed

blanket

book

bookcase

CD

CD-player

ceiling

chest of drawers

clock

comb

comic

computer

curtains

cushion

dice

doll

door handle

dressing gown

duvet

floor

What do you have in your bedroom?

letter

model plane

picture

postcard

rug

slippers

toy car

toy train

light switch

photo

pillow

radiator

sheet

teddy bear

toy rocket

wall

game

hairbrush

jigsaw

lamp

wardrobe

window

In the workshop

battery

bolt

cardboard

clip

gloves

hammer

inventor

light bulb

blowtorch

calculator

chisel

drill

goggles

handle

keyboard

machine

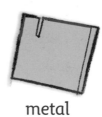

mask

metal

monitor

mouse

oil can

overalls

paper

penknife

pliers

printer

robot

sandpaper

saw

screw

screwdriver

shelf

spanner

tape measure

teaspoon

mug

nail

nut

oil

wire

wood

In the street

bike

boy

bridge

buggy

bungalow

car

chimney

crossroads

doorbell

fence

fire engine

flat

flowerpot

garden

girl

greenhouse

hosepipe

house

ladder

minibus

What colour is the car at the traffic lights?

playground

road

roof

school

scooter

shed

shop

streetlight

taxi

traffic lights

tree

tricycle

truck

vegetables

washing line

motorbike

pavement

pelican crossing

pigeon

watering can

zebra crossing

13

At school

abcdef
ghijklm
nopqrs
tuvwxyz

alphabet

book

box

clay

cupboard

display

drawing pin

globe

crayon

desk

drawer

felt-tip pen

glue

hook

library

magnet

model

notepad

paint

What do you like doing at school?

Our shells

$1 + 4 = 5$

pencil sharpener

plant

poster

pot

rubber

ruler

sandpit

scissors

stapler

sticker

sticky tape

table

teacher

wastepaper basket

paintbrush

painting

pen

pencil

whiteboard

xylophone

15

In the town

How many buses can you see?

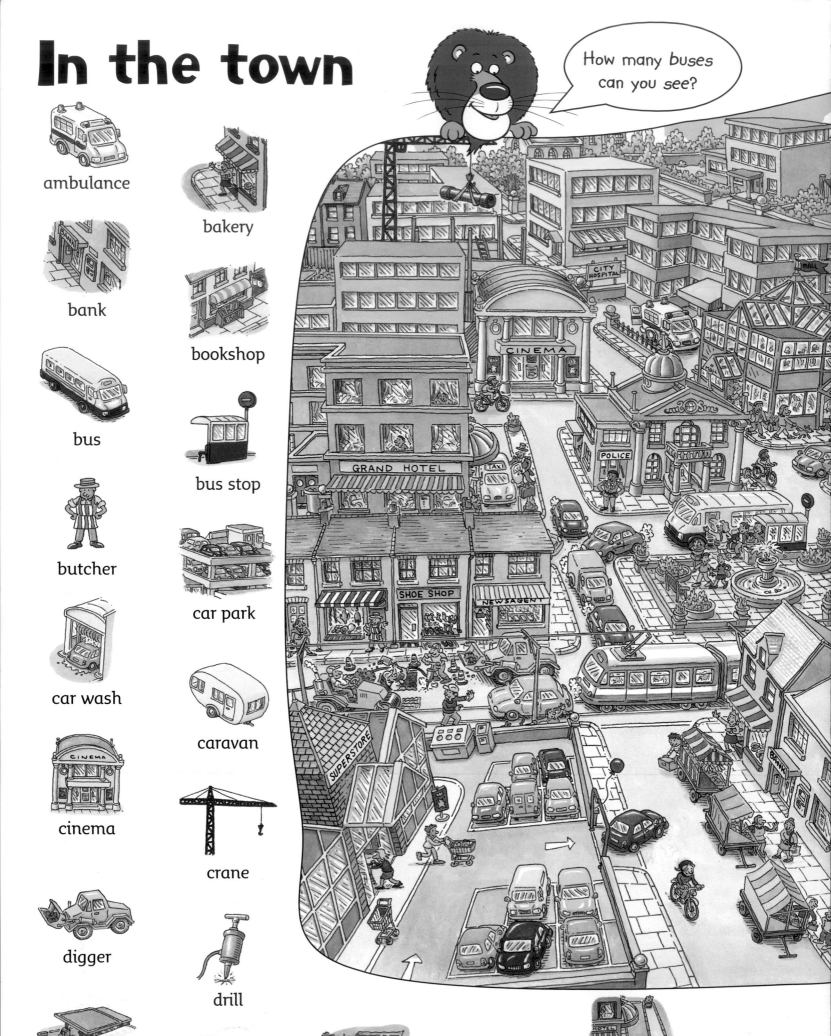

ambulance

bank

bus

butcher

car wash

cinema

digger

filling station

bakery

bookshop

bus stop

car park

caravan

crane

drill

fire station

hole

hospital

hotel

library

16

pipe

police station

restaurant

roadworks

shopping centre

supermarket

theatre

park

petrol pump

police officer

post office

roadroller

shoe shop

spade

swimming pool

town hall

market

newsagent

nursery

offices

traffic jam

tram

17

Let's go shopping

apple

bar code

bread

butter

carrier bag

cereal

cheese

chocolate

banana

biscuits

broccoli

can

carrot

checkout

chicken

cucumber

eggs

fish

freezer

grapes

How many people are carrying shopping baskets?

mushroom

mop

onion

orange

pear

pineapple

potato

scales

shop assistant

shopping basket

shopping trolley

sign

strawberry

till

tomato

juice

lemon

meat

milk

washing powder

washing-up liquid

At the doctor's

blind

coat hook

cotton wool

doctor

form

bandage

magazine

notice board

office

prescription

reception desk

receptionist

scales

sticking plaster

tissues

toys

umbrella

waiting room

walking stick

At the hospital

bed

card

chart

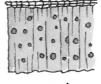
crutches

curtain

injection

medicine

nurse

plaster cast

stethoscope

stitches

stretcher

syringe

tablets

Have you ever been to hospital?

thermometer

tray

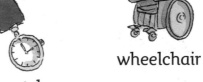
trolley

watch

wheelchair

x-ray

21

At the vet

basket

beak

bedding

bowl

budgie

cage

collar

feather

fish tank

gerbil

goldfish

guinea pig

hamster

kitten

lead

mouse

paw

puppy

rabbit

rat

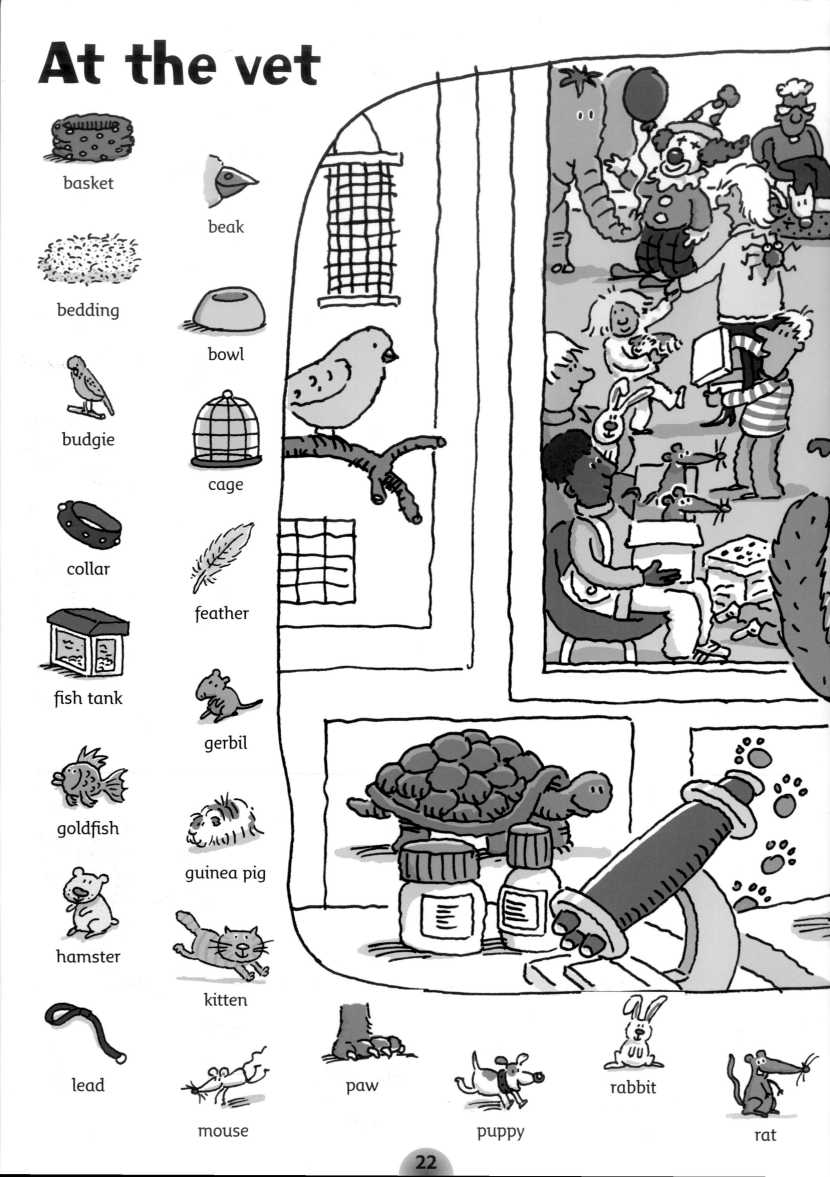

snake

spider

tail

tortoise

vet

wing

At the park

baby

balloon

band

bandstand

bat

bench

bin

bird

climbing frame

dog

duck

flowers

football

gardener

gates

goose

grass

helmet

hot-air balloon

kiosk

What do you like to do at the park?

24

picnic

pond

rollerblades

rowing boat

playing field

race

roundabout

see-saw

skateboard

slide

swan

sign

skipping rope

squirrel

swing

tree

kite

lawnmower

leaves

path

tennis

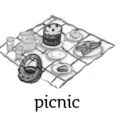

Going on a journey

airport

barrier

carriage

engine

flight attendant

glider

handbag

lift

bag

café

clock

escalator

fork-lift truck

guidebook

helicopter

menu

mobile phone

money

napkin

pilot

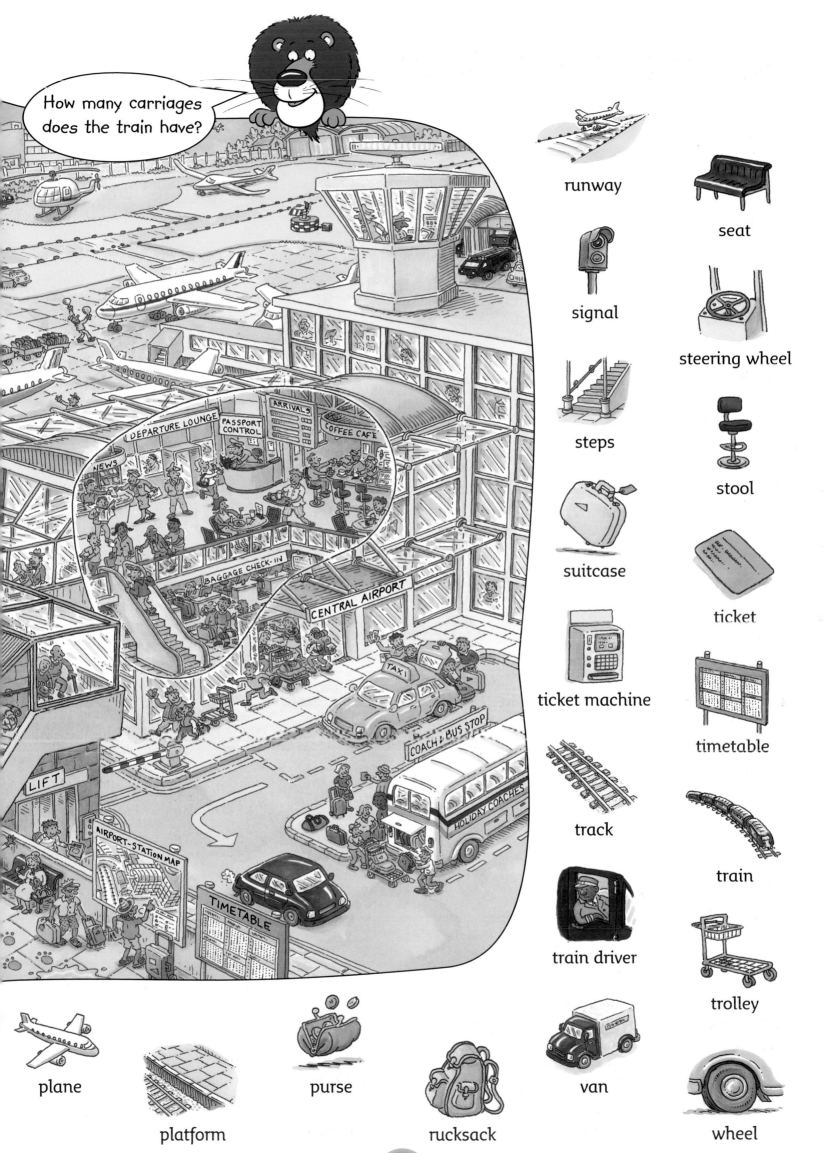

How many carriages does the train have?

runway

signal

steps

suitcase

ticket machine

track

train driver

van

seat

steering wheel

stool

ticket

timetable

train

trolley

wheel

plane

platform

purse

rucksack

On the farm

barn

brush

bucket

bull

burrow

calf

cat

chick

combine harvester

cow

crow

farmer

farmhouse

farmyard

field

foal

fork

gate

goat

hay

lamb

mice

What animal gives us wool?

nest

plough

sack

saddle

scarecrow

sheep

sky

stable

stile

straw

tractor

trough

tyre

wheat

haystack

horse

kids

wheelbarrow

worm

hen

In the countryside

ant

bee

beetle

branch

cable car

caterpillar

dragonfly

fly

badger

beehive

butterfly

canoe

deer

fish

forest

fox

frog

frogspawn

grasshopper

hedgehog

What do you like to do in the countryside?

narrow boat

rabbit

robin

snail

tadpole

toad

wasp

windmill

mountain

owl

river

slug

stepping stones

tent

village

waterfall

woodpecker

hill

ladybird

lake

mole

At the beach

How many *seagulls* can you *see*?

ball

bucket

camera

cliff

crab

deckchair

dinghy

ferry

fishing rod

flipper

harbour

ice cream

ice cream van

ice lolly

lifeguard

lighthouse

net

oar

pebble

pier

seagull

seaweed

shell

snorkel

spade

speedboat

starfish

sun hat

sunglasses

sunscreen

sunshade

surfboard

swimming costume

swimming trunks

towel

wave

rock pool

sandcastle

sea

windsurfer

yacht

sand

Pirate Island

anchor

barrel

beach

cave

chain

chest

coconut

coins

crocodile

dolphin

elephant

giraffe

gold

gorilla

hippo

jungle

lion

jellyfish

kangaroo

lizard

Can you find the hidden treasure?

parrot

pirate captain

rock

shark

skeleton

telescope

treasure

palm tree

pirate

rhino

sail

ship

sword

tiger

turtle

volcano

lobster

map

monkey

octopus

whale

35

Jobs we do

actor

artist

astronaut

author

baker

builder

bus driver

butcher

carpenter

dancer

dentist

doctor

electrician

farmer

firefighter

flight attendant

footballer

gardener

hairdresser

judge   lawyer

librarian

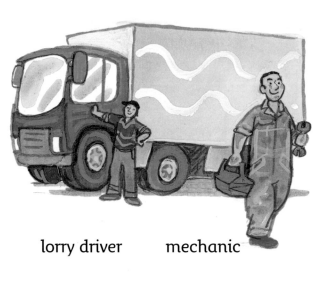

lorry driver   mechanic

musician

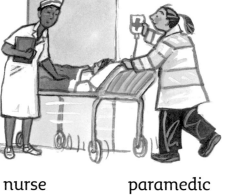

nurse   paramedic

photographer

pilot

plumber

police officer

pop star

postman

reporter

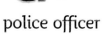

scientist

secretary

shopkeeper

teacher

train driver

TV presenter

waiter

What does a builder do?

My body

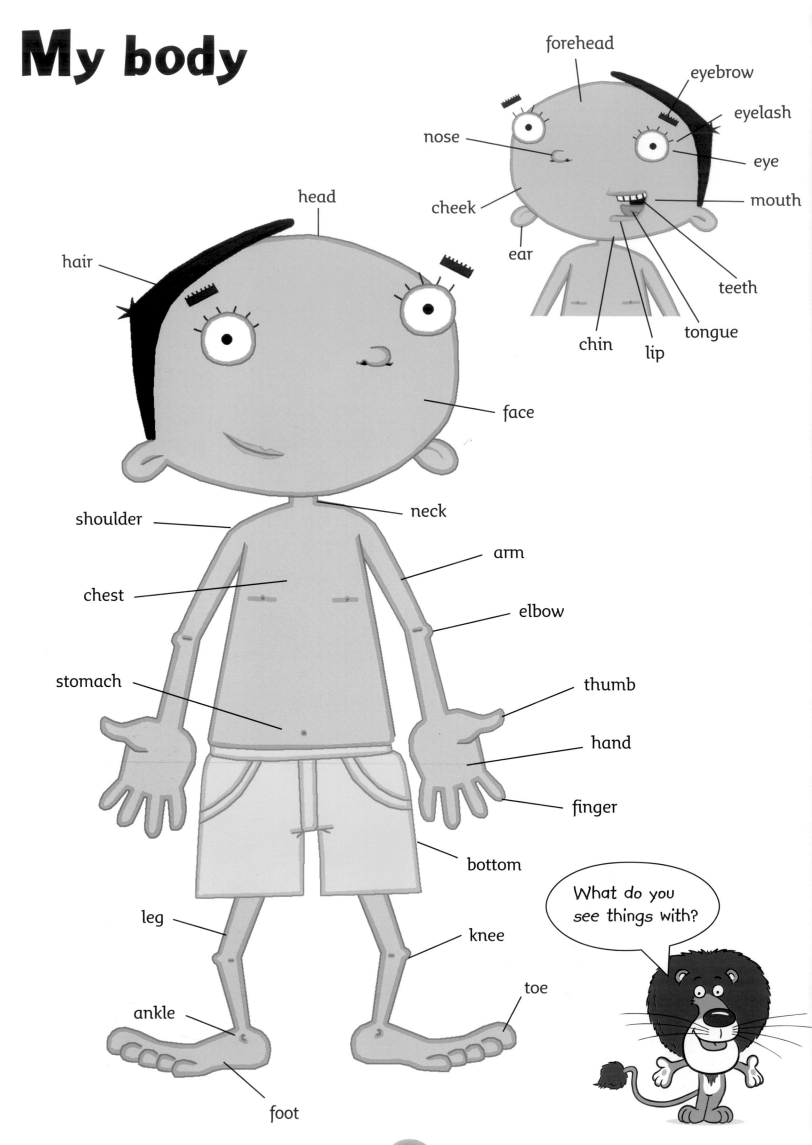

forehead

eyebrow

eyelash

nose

eye

mouth

cheek

head

teeth

ear

tongue

chin

lip

hair

face

neck

shoulder

arm

chest

elbow

stomach

thumb

hand

finger

bottom

What do you *see* things with?

leg

knee

toe

ankle

foot

My family

mother

father

sister

brother

grandmother

grandfather

uncle

aunt

niece

nephew

Clothes

What do you like to wear?

coat

sunglasses

socks

dressing gown

tie

watch

trainers

gloves

T-shirt

pocket

belt

shorts

buckle

trousers

pants

flip-flops

vest

pyjamas

scarf

shirt

blouse

hat

nightgown

glasses

shoes

boots

necklace

skirt

button

cardigan

dress

tights

jacket

sandals

waterproof

jeans

jumper

knickers

41

Seasons

spring

summer

Weather

sunny

cloudy

foggy

rainy

windy

snowy

autumn

winter

breeze

gale

rainbow

lightning

thunder

storm

frosty

icy

What weather do you like best?

Food and meals

cereal

coffee

egg

honey

jam

breakfast

salt

sugar

tea

toast

juice

milk

pepper

porridge

yogurt

cake

chips

curry

fruit salad

hamburger

jelly

noodles

peas

baked potato

bread roll

chicken

crisps

What do you like to eat?

lunch

fish

fruit

pasta

salad

sandwiches

dinner

pizza

potatoes

quiche

rice

sauce

sausages

steak

stir fry

45

Numbers

1 one
2 two
3 three
4 four
5 five
6 six
7 seven
8 eight
9 nine
10 ten
11 eleven
12 twelve
13 thirteen
14 fourteen
15 fifteen
16 sixteen
17 seventeen
18 eighteen
19 nineteen
20 twenty

1st first
3rd third
2nd second
4th fourth

How many brushes are there?

5th fifth   **7th** seventh   **9th** ninth   **11th** eleventh

6th sixth   **8th** eighth   **10th** tenth   **12th** twelfth

Colours and shapes

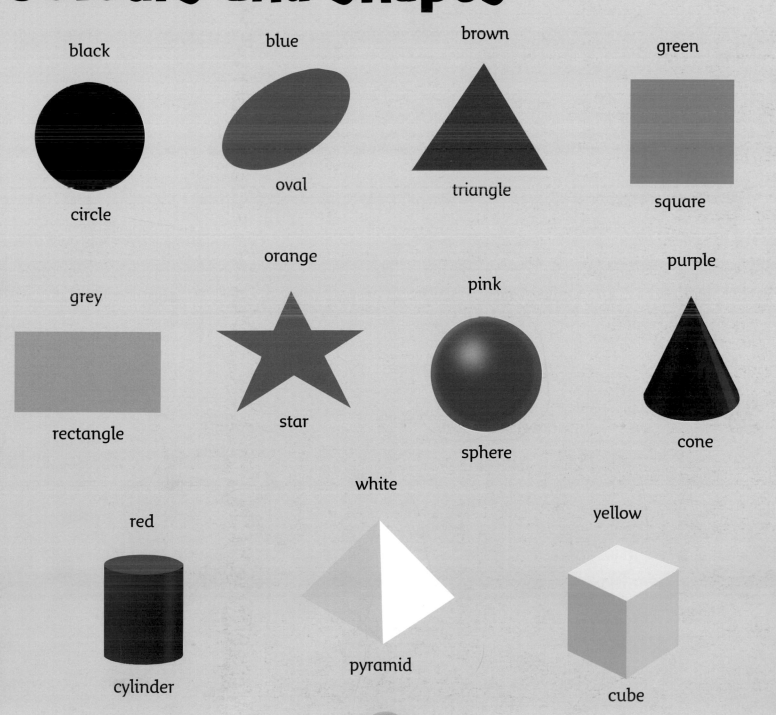

black

circle

blue

oval

brown

triangle

green

square

grey

rectangle

orange

star

pink

sphere

purple

cone

red

cylinder

white

pyramid

yellow

cube

49

Months

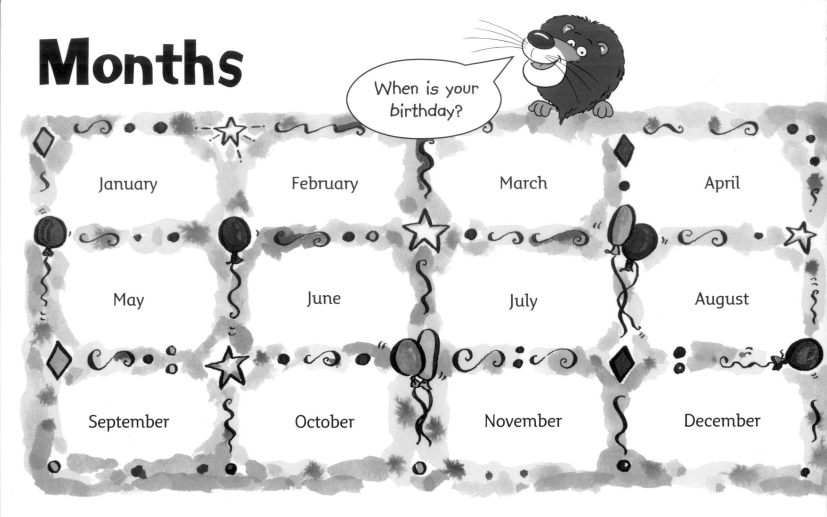

When is your birthday?

January	February	March	April
May	June	July	August
September	October	November	December

Days of the week

Monday

Tuesday

Wednesday

Thursday

Friday

Saturday

Sunday

Times of the day

morning

midday

afternoon

evening

night

midnight

Telling the time

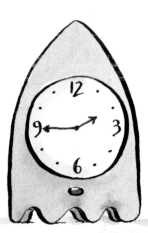

one o'clock
1:00

quarter past one
1:15

half past one
1:30

quarter to two
1:45

two o'clock
2:00

Opposites

asleep awake

big small

clean dirty

come go

dark light

fast slow

few many

front back

full empty

heavy light

high low

hot cold

loud quiet

old   new

soft   hard

tidy   messy

wet   dry

wide   narrow

What is the opposite of fast?

Position words

top

above

first

far

up

down

last

between

behind

in front

beside

below

over

on

off

bottom

under

near

Animals

bird

cat

Miaow!

cow

Moo!

dog

Woof!

donkey

duck

Quack!

elephant

frog

goose

horse

insects

Buzz!

lion

mouse

owl

sheep

Baa!

zebra

What sound does a frog make?

54

Things we say

Words we use a lot

a	going	said
all	he	see
am	I	she
and	in	the
are	is	they
at	it	this
away	like	to
can	look	up
come	me	was
day	my	we
for	of	went
get	on	you
go	play	your

Index

Go to page 5 to find out how to use the index.

potatoes 45
pour 47
prescription 20
printer 11
pull 47
puppy 22
purple 49
purse 27
push 47
pyjamas 40
pyramid 49

Qq
quack 54
quarter past one 51
quarter to two 51
quiche 45
quiet 52

Rr
rabbit 22, 31
race 25
radiator 9
radio 7
rainy 42
rainbow 43
rat 23
read 47
reception desk 20
receptionist 20
rectangle 49
red 49
reporter 37
restaurant 17
rhino 35
rice 45
ride 47
ring 41
river 31
road 13
roadroller 17
roadworks 17
robin 31
robot 11
rock 35

rock pool 33
rollerblades 25
roof 13
roundabout 25
rowing boat 25
rubber 15
rucksack 27
rug 9
ruler 15
run 47
runway 27

Ss
sack 29
saddle 29
said 55
sail 35
salad 45
salt 44
sand 33
sandals 41
sandcastle 33
sandpaper 11
sandpit 15
sandwiches 45
Saturday 50
sauce 45
sausages 45
saw 11
scales 19, 20
scarecrow 29
scarf 40
school 14
scientist 37
scissors 15
scooter 13
screw 11
screwdriver 11
sea 33
seagull 33
seat 27
seaweed 33
second 48
secretary 37
see 55

see you 55
see-saw 25
September 50
seven 48
seventeen 48
seventh 49
shampoo 7
shark 35
she 55
shed 13
sheep 29, 54
sheet 9
shelf 11
shell 33
ship 35
shirt 40
shoe shop 17
shoes 41
shop 13
shop assistant 19
shopkeeper 37
shopping centre 17
shopping trolley 19
shorts 40
shoulder 38
shout 47
shower 7, 42
sign 19, 25
signal 27
sing 47
sink 7
sister 39
sit 47
six 48
sixteen 48
sixth 49
skateboard 25
skeleton 35
skip 47
skipping rope 25
skirt 41
sky 29
slide 25
slippers 9
slow 52

Answers to Big Cat's questions

Did you answer my questions? Look for the page number and *see* if you were right.

page 6: You clean your teeth in the bathroom.

page 11: There are nine screws.

page 13: The car at the traffic lights is red.

page 16: There are two buses.

page 19: There are four people carrying shopping baskets.

page 23: The hamster is sitting on a boy's head.

page 27: The train has three carriages (and two engines).

page 29: Sheep give us wool.

page 32: There are nine seagulls at the beach.

page 35: The treasure is hidden in the cave.

page 37: A builder builds houses and other buildings.

page 38: You *see* things with your eyes.

page 47: There are eight balls.

page 48: There are seventeen brushes.

page 53: The opposite of fast is slow.